AMERICAN REVOLUTIONARIES AND FOUNDERS OF THE NATION

Other titles in the **Collective Biographies** *series*

Collective Biographies

AMERICAN REVOLUTIONARIES AND FOUNDERS OF THE NATION

James Meisner, Jr., and Amy Ruth

Enslow Publishers, Inc.

40 Industrial Road	PO Box 38
Box 398	Aldershot
Berkeley Heights, NJ 07922	Hants GU12 6BP
USA	UK

http://www.enslow.com

Library of Congress Cataloging-in-Publication Data

Meisner, James.
    American revolutionaries and Founders of the nation / James
Meisner, Jr., and Amy Ruth.
        p. cm. — (Collective biographies)
    Includes bibliographical references and index.
    Summary: Discusses the lives of John Adams, John Jay, Thomas
Jefferson, Alexander Hamilton, James Madison, George Mason, William
Paterson, Roger Sherman, Gouverneur Morris, and Richard Henry Lee.
    ISBN 0-7660-1115-1
    1. Statesmen—United States—Biography—Juvenile literature.
    2. Presidents—United States—Biography—Juvenile literature.
    3. United States—Politics and government—1775–1783—Juvenile
literature. 4. United States—Politics and government—1783–1809—
Juvenile literature. [1. Statesmen. 2. Presidents. 3. United
States—Politics and government—1775–1783. 4. United States—
Politics and government—1783–1809] I. Ruth, Amy. II. Title.
III. Series.
E302.5.M44   1999
973.4'092'2
[B]—DC21   98-30351
                                                    CIP
                                                    AC

Printed in the United States of America

10 9 8 7 6 5 4 3 2 1

To Our Readers: All Internet addresses in this book were active and appropriate
when we went to press. Any comments or suggestions can be sent by e-mail to
Comments@enslow.com or to the address on the back cover.

Illustration Credits: John Grafton, *The American Revolution: A Picture Sourcebook*,
New York: Dover Publications, Inc., 1975, p. 6, 55; National Archives and Records
Administration, pp. 14, 24, 40, 46, 52, 62, 70, 80, 95, 102; Reproduced from the
Collections of the Library of Congress, pp. 20, 30, 34, 42, 68, 76, 84, 98; The
William Paterson University of New Jersey, p. 88.

Cover Illustration: Architect of the Capitol (shows the signing of the Constitution)

Contents

Introduction

In the United States people have the freedom to pray, live, and think as they choose. It hasn't always been this way. More than two hundred years ago the nation's founding fathers earned the freedoms we take for granted today.

But the creation of a new nation didn't take place overnight or even in just a few short years.

The first permanent European colony in North America was established at Jamestown, Virginia, in 1607. The Pilgrims settled Plymouth, Massachusetts, thirteen years later. Other colonies soon followed. Some were established as moneymaking ventures. Others were created as havens for religious freedom.

Over the years, France, Spain, and England vied for dominance over the New World. These countries fought several wars to gain control over the vast natural resources the land offered. For more than 145 years, people in what would become the United States worked and lived as British subjects in separate and isolated colonies. But by the 1750s, some of these people were calling for some sort of union of the colonies. This was a unique idea in a unique land.

The philosophical roots of this idea began with the republic of ancient Greece. These roots trace their way through the Enlightenment period of the late 1600s. The Enlightenment challenged old ideas and encouraged new ways of thinking. The founding fathers borrowed these ideas to create a new form of representative government.

These men assumed roles of leadership when they were most needed. They were busy living their lives as students, soldiers, lawyers, farmers, and writers—one was even a shoemaker. They had no idea they would one day help build a new nation.

Between 1764 and 1767, Great Britain passed a series of laws and taxes that applied only to British subjects living in the colonies. The colonists felt that these taxes, such as the Currency Act and the Stamp Act, were a violation of their rights as British citizens. Colonists began to realize that what was good for the king and Great Britain wasn't always good for the people of the colonies. In response to these new taxes, the colonists began to question the government. From 1765 to 1776, more than four hundred pamphlets were written by the colonists. Most pamphlets criticized the king, and some urged revolution and independence.

The call for independence grew louder after five townspeople were killed in the Boston Massacre of 1770. British troops were sent to the city to enforce the king's unpopular laws. They fired on an unarmed mob in the streets of Boston. The deaths shocked many colonists.

Finally, after years of discussion, fifty-six representatives from across the colonies met in September 1774. They considered forming a Continental Association. Some leaders, like Virginia's

Richard Henry Lee, were ready for a completely new government. Most colonists wanted to repair the relationship with the king and remain British subjects.

Colonial delegates met again in 1775. British troops and the Massachusetts militia had fought in Lexington and Concord. But many delegates to the Second Continental Congress still didn't want to break with Great Britain. Congress finally listened to Lee's urgings only after the king rejected the "Olive Branch Petition."

In 1776, the Continental Congress passed a Declaration of Independence. Delegates declared openly for the first time "That these United Colonies are, and of Right ought to be Free and Independent States."

The founding fathers took a serious risk. Had they lost the war, they would have faced the possibility of execution. The founding fathers felt so strongly about the cause of freedom that in the last line of the Declaration they pledged "to each other our Lives, our Fortunes and our sacred Honor."

The Congress led the colonies through the Revolutionary War without a written constitution or national courts. It wasn't until March 1, 1781, that the Articles of Confederation were finally adopted. The Articles allowed each state one vote, giving equal voting power to large and small states. The Articles didn't give Congress the power to pass trade laws or to raise money. The war was very expensive, and debt soon became a national issue.

Because the Articles of Confederation were so weak, the national government was also weak. Many of the founding fathers returned to their homes where they worked drafting individual state constitutions. In their home states they learned how constitutions should be written. When the Constitutional Convention met in 1787 in Philadelphia's State House (now called Independence Hall), the delegates were prepared.

Like the Annapolis Convention several months before, the National Convention of 1787 was called to discuss commerce. Most of the fifty-five delegates were ready to talk about other important issues, too.

In the preamble to the Constitution, the founding fathers explained the need "to form a more perfect Union." However, the nation in 1787 was less than a perfect union. There was a world of difference between the wealthy upper class and the middle class of artisans and shop owners. At the lower end of the social ladder were the slaves whose unpaid labor helped build the New World.

Slavery existed in every colony. In 1776, for example, one out of every seven New Yorkers was a slave. Thomas Jefferson tried to criticize slavery in the Declaration of Independence. But South Carolina and Georgia opposed his effort. Sympathetic northern states who still participated in the slave trade also disagreed with Jefferson. His references to slavery were edited out before the final document.

New Yorkers John Jay and Alexander Hamilton and Virginian James Madison believed that a strong national government was important to the future of the colonies. Others, like New Jersey's William Paterson and Virginia's Jefferson, encouraged stronger state governments. As the new nation developed, supporters of both types of government found themselves at odds.

Most of the continent's great minds met in the spring of 1787 to test their philosophies and draft the national constitution. Those who were absent contributed their thoughts in letters to their friends. The men's different philosophies and personalities caused conflict all summer long. Small states feared being overpowered by large states. Old friendships were strained, and new alliances were made.

These feelings didn't disappear after the delegates signed the new Constitution. Virginia's Richard Henry Lee and George Mason opposed the adoption of the Constitution. They argued that the Constitution didn't specifically protect the rights of individuals. In response to their complaints, the Bill of Rights was added as the first ten amendments to the Constitution.

The founding fathers used many sources to write the Declaration of Independence and the Constitution. They looked to British common law and modern and ancient political theories. They also called upon their years of education and their own daily experiences. The Constitution is called a "living document" because it allows future generations to peaceably change the government. The founding fathers knew that as daily experiences changed, the nation's laws would need to reflect these changes. Today, original copies of the Declaration of Independence and the Constitution are displayed in the National Archives in Washington, D.C.

But just as books are more than paper and ink, the birth of the United States was more than the Declaration of Independence, the Revolutionary War, and the Constitution. The founding fathers established a new country. Many assumed roles of responsibility in the new government. They served as foreign diplomats, as representatives to Congress, and as presidents.

The strong philosophies that helped found the nation also helped form political parties. The Federalist and Democratic-Republican parties reflected the deep beliefs of these early lawmakers. Federalists supported a strong federal government. Democratic-Republicans advocated a weak federal government. These same ideas live on in today's modern political parties.

The following biographies honor the men who helped found the United States of America. John Adams was the voice of the independence movement. John Jay was slow to support independence, but his sharp legal mind helped lead the new nation in the proper direction. Thomas Jefferson wrote the Declaration of Independence. As president, he served as a bridge between the nation's early days and its bright future. Alexander Hamilton rose from absolute poverty to become the nation's first secretary of the treasury. James Madison created the blueprint for the Constitution. George Mason placed the rights of the individual above all else. William Paterson was an early supporter of independence and the rights of the states over a national government. Roger Sherman, one of the first "career politicians," held more offices than any other founding father. Gouverneur Morris supported the new nation and personally wrote the words in the final version of the Constitution. Richard Henry Lee led the independence movement. Even though he opposed adoption of the Constitution, he supported the Bill of Rights.

Each man carried in him the spirit of freedom and independence that started with the Declaration of Independence and lives on today in the nation they helped build.

John Adams

1

John Adams

The Voice of Independence

John Adams had a choice to make. He knew that his abrupt style offended some of his fellow delegates. However, he was appointed to the committee responsible for drafting the Declaration of Independence in 1776. Adams knew that the delegates might oppose independence simply because he was involved. He refused to write the Declaration and instead handed the pen to thirty-three-year-old Thomas Jefferson. Jefferson went on to produce one of the most important documents in the history of the United States.

John Adams was born on October 30, 1735, at Braintree (now Quincy), Massachusetts. The oldest of three sons born to John Adams, Sr., and Susanna Boylston, young John shared the family's strong

Puritan beliefs. Like other ordinary children, he had many varied interests. "I spent my time as idle Children do in making and sailing boats and Ships upon the Ponds and Brooks, in making and flying Kites, in driving hoops, playing marbles," Adams wrote in his autobiography.[1]

John disliked his public school teacher. "I cared not what I did if I could but get away from school, and confess to my shame that I sometimes play'd truant," he remembered years later.[2] Because he didn't like his teacher, John was sent to private schools. He studied with several tutors before he finally learned to enjoy education.

A nervous Adams eventually took and passed the entrance tests to Harvard University. This fulfilled his father's dream to send his firstborn son to college. Adams graduated at nineteen. His family expected him to study theology and become a minister. After teaching school for a year, however, Adams decided that he would rather be a lawyer. He taught and studied law for two years, and in 1758 Adams was allowed to practice law.

A few years later, in his hometown of Braintree, Adams met sixteen-year-old Abigail Smith and fell deeply in love. Her family believed that he was socially beneath her and opposed their relationship. Adams pursued her for nearly four years, and they finally married on October 25, 1764.

John and Abigail loved each other deeply. In a time when women were considered inferior to men,

John and Abigail treated each other as intellectual equals. They were married for fifty-four years. Together they had six children, including a future president, John Quincy Adams.

Many of the Massachusetts residents of the day were religious conservatives. A Unitarian, Adams was no different. A deeply religious man, Adams's conservative beliefs influenced his daily actions and his political philosophies.

Like many of the other founding fathers, Adams was very ambitious. He also had a darker, envious side that made him outspoken, blunt, and insulting. If he couldn't succeed or excel, he resented those who did, friend and foe alike. His driving envy influenced his actions for his entire life.

His strong personality often turned friends into political and personal enemies, including Alexander Hamilton and Thomas Jefferson. Sometimes, though, his strong sense of humor helped him win over potential enemies.

As an ambitious Massachusetts lawyer, Adams opposed the Stamp Act and represented local patriots held by the British. He also successfully defended the British soldiers accused of shooting unarmed civilians during the Boston Massacre.

As a port city and colonial capital, Boston was a major city in the days before the revolution. So by the time he was named a delegate to the First Continental Congress in 1774, Adams already was a respected leader of the independence movement.

Between 1774 and 1777, Adams served on ninety committees. He was a member of the committee that drafted the Declaration of Independence, which he helped edit. He chaired twenty-five committees, including the Board of War, which directed the operations of the revolution.

The vote for independence was passed on July 2. The final Declaration was edited and debated for two days until July 4. Adams uncorrectly assumed that Independence Day would be celebrated on July 2. In a letter to Abigail, Adams wrote,

> I am apt to believe that it will be celebrated, by succeeding Generations, as the great anniversary Festival. . . . It ought to be solemnized with Pomp and Parade, with Shews, Games, Sports, Guns, Bells, Bonfires and Illuminations from one End of this Continent to the other from this Time forward forever more.[3]

Congress named Adams a minister to France in February 1778. Travel was extremely dangerous for a well-known revolutionary like Adams, so he made his arrangements in secret. Very few of his friends and business associates knew of his plans until after he had gone. After secretly slipping out of Braintree and sailing away under the watchful eyes of the British warships, Adams entered France.

For the next nine years, Adams repeatedly made the two-month-long journey across the Atlantic Ocean. He traveled from his beloved New England to fulfill his responsibilities as an official representative of the new nation. Adams negotiated trade agreements with several governments in Europe. He also helped strengthen the new nation by securing loans.

Adams helped draft the Massachusetts State Constitution in 1779. The constitution was drafted by a committee and submitted to the people for approval, a process the United States Constitution would follow several years later.

In June 1781, five months before the British surrendered at Yorktown, Adams led the five-member commission responsible for negotiating peace with Great Britain. After long and complex negotiations, the commissioners signed the Treaty of Paris on September 3, 1783.

On February 24, 1785, Adams became the first American envoy to London. This was a very long way to travel for one of America's first and more vocal supporters of independence.

In his many letters to his wife, Adams repeatedly wrote that he wanted to be home with her. Adams finally returned to Braintree in April 1788. He spent the rest of the year unpacking and settling into the house he had bought the previous fall.

Congress elected Adams vice-president under George Washington in March 1789. Even by today's standards, Adams would be considered overweight. Some of his political foes jokingly called him "His Rotundity."[4]

As an official representative of a newly-formed nation, Adams traveled all over Europe.

Two of the three branches of government were in place—Congress and the presidency. In April 1789, Adams presided over the Senate in the first session of the First Congress.

Adams was reelected vice-president in 1792. Together with other founding fathers, Adams helped put into practice the new form of government they had begun with the Declaration of Independence in 1776.

In 1796, Adams, backed by the Federalist party, ran for president against Thomas Jefferson. Jefferson represented the Democratic-Republican party. In the twenty years since they had worked together on the Declaration of Independence, the two men had developed very different political views. Jefferson believed that most political power should rest with the states. Adams thought that the federal government should have the greater control.

In the first contested presidential election, Adams was elected president. Jefferson finished second and was elected vice-president. Their different political beliefs made it difficult for Adams and Jefferson to work together. Congress eventually moved to change the Constitution to ensure that a similar election result would not happen again.

Because of their different visions for the future of the new nation, Adams often clashed with fellow Federalist Alexander Hamilton. Hamilton tried to prevent Adams's election to the presidency and afterward worked against his administration.

By 1798, Adams's policies had helped prevent a war with France, but Hamilton and his supporters finally broke with Adams. At the same time, the enactment of the Alien and Sedition Acts further angered Jefferson and his supporters. The Alien and Sedition Acts were directed against foreigners and critics of the government.

Adams helped move the seat of government from Philadelphia to Washington, D.C. In November 1800, he became the first president to sleep in the Executive Mansion, now called the White House. In the election two months later, the split between Adams and Hamilton prevented Adams from receiving a majority of the votes. Jefferson defeated Adams and became the third president.

In the first peaceful yet involuntary change of power between political parties in the United States, Adams demonstrated to the world that the Constitution was more important than the political wishes of a losing politician. Adams stepped down, and he and Abigail retired to their home in Massachusetts.

Adams lived to see his son John Quincy Adams elected the sixth president of the United States in 1824. John Adams died on July 4, 1826, the anniversary of the nation he helped found.

Although his last words were "Jefferson still survives," his old friend, compatriot, and political rival had actually preceded him in death by several hours. The voice of independence was silent.

2

Alexander Hamilton
Founding Federalist

Alexander Hamilton overcame a troubled and desperate childhood to become one of the new nation's financial leaders. Today he is one of only a handful of the founding fathers honored on United States currency.

Hamilton's mother, Rachel Lavine, left her husband and a young son to live with Scottish merchant James Hamilton in the islands of the West Indies. Alexander was born January 11, 1755, on the island of Nevis. He and his parents, also with their first son, James Jr., settled in St. Croix. James Hamilton soon deserted both children and their mother. He left them penniless and alone.

Rachel opened a general store and saw to young Alexander's education, but she died when he was

Alexander Hamilton

eleven. Intensely intelligent, Alexander served as a merchant's clerk. He quickly developed an ability for business and management. Hamilton never forgot his poor childhood and was ambitious all his life.

In 1772, a Presbyterian minister read a letter Hamilton had published in the local newspaper. Impressed with the bright young man, the minister helped raise money to send Hamilton to America to continue his formal education.

Hamilton attended a preparatory school in New Jersey, and in 1774 he entered King's College in New York City, today known as Columbia University. He studied medicine, but his interests soon turned to mathematics, politics, and writing. From December 1774 to February 1775, twenty-year-old Hamilton published a series of pamphlets that defined the political theories that would guide his political life.

His pamphlets caught the eye of fellow New Yorker John Jay, who was serving in the Continental Congress in Philadelphia. Hamilton exchanged many letters with Jay, informing him of events back home.[1]

The spring of 1775 found the colonies preparing for war. Although the drafting of the Declaration of Independence was still a year away, Hamilton joined a militia company. In the militia he divided his time between the drills of soldiers and the demands of the classroom. Hamilton worked his way up through the ranks as a volunteer, drilling every morning before classes. In March 1776, he was appointed commander of the company of artillery responsible for protecting New York City.

Captain Hamilton commanded his men courageously in several battles. Soon he earned the attention of General George Washington, the commander of the army. In March 1777, Hamilton became Washington's special aide. He also received a promotion to the rank of lieutenant colonel.

As his military career blossomed, his personal life, too, took a turn for the better. In December 1780, Hamilton married Elizabeth Schuyler, the daughter of an influential and wealthy New York family.

Hamilton excelled as Washington's primary letter writer and clerk. But after a few years he grew tired of Washington's bad temper and sought his own command. Hamilton resigned his position to return to the front lines. He led the final charge against the British at Yorktown, Virginia, in October 1781. Leading his soldiers in the dangerous night attack, Hamilton won the battle and cleared the road to America's independence.

Although Hamilton had surpassed his humble position as a merchant's clerk, he had long ago learned that money would decide his and the new nation's future. After his tremendous success at Yorktown, Hamilton left the army and studied law. The young lawyer's war record and his views on banking and money earned him a job as the New York Receiver of Continental Taxes. Hamilton was responsible for collecting the taxes New York owed to the Continental Congress, but he lacked any enforcement authority. Not surprisingly, he had very little success.

Later in 1782, Hamilton was elected to the Continental Congress. For eight months, he battled the status quo of the Articles of Confederation. He was angry with the inability of Congress to pay the soldiers. Also, Congress had a growing debt after the war and there were no plans for the future prosperity or security of the states. Hamilton left Congress in the summer of 1783. He and his family moved into a house in Manhattan.

Hamilton worked hard at his legal business. He helped found the Bank of New York, and with founding fathers John Jay and Gouverneur Morris, he helped form an antislavery society.

In 1786, Hamilton was elected to the New York legislature. He also served as a delegate to the Annapolis Convention. At the end of the four-day meeting, Hamilton drafted the convention's address. The document urged the states to meet again and create a plan that would ensure the future of the federal government.

As a soldier, Hamilton helped the new nation secure its independence. In Annapolis he set in motion events that would define the new nation.

In May 1787, Hamilton was one of three New York delegates sent to Philadelphia for the Constitutional Convention. Hamilton had very little influence at the convention because his two fellow

New York delegates opposed a strong national government. Hamilton didn't speak for nearly a month and contributed very little to the text of the new constitution.

Finally, on June 18, 1787, Hamilton rose and delivered his vision of the future government. He spoke for five hours and shocked those in attendance. He offered radical suggestions, including lifelong terms for the chief executive and members of the senate. He also supported the appointment of the state governors by the national government. Hamilton proposed taking national steps far beyond those called for in the Virginia Plan. His ideas frightened delegates from smaller states and failed to influence delegates from larger states. For the next two weeks, Hamilton joined Madison in support of several proposals that favored the federal government over the individual states.

On June 30, Hamilton left the convention and returned home to attend to legal business. When he returned after an absence of more than a month, he continued to disagree with the direction of the proceedings but said very little. Hamilton told his fellow delegates that he had remained silent because of his "dislike of the Scheme of Govt. in General."[2] Despite his dislike, Hamilton signed the final version of the Constitution. He was the only New York delegate to do so.

The Constitution reflected the beliefs of the delegates but lacked a bill of rights. It still had a long way to go before becoming the law of the land. Fearing that the only other choice would be no national government at all, Hamilton worked hard to secure New York's approval.

Along with friends John Jay and James Madison, Hamilton began writing a series of essays in support of the Constitution. The essays were originally published in New York and Virginia newspapers. *The Federalist* papers, as they came to be called, eventually were collected into a publication distributed across the colonies. Hamilton wrote fifty-two of the eighty-five essays, which set forth his political beliefs. Together, *The Federalist* papers served as the blueprint for political thought in the United States for the next two hundred years.

Once the Constitution was adopted, Hamilton worked to ensure the election of George Washington and John Adams as president and vice-president.

On September 11, 1789, Washington named Hamilton the first secretary of the treasury. Hamilton again found himself as an advisor to Washington. His support of an expansive federal government often put him at odds with others in Washington's cabinet, including Secretary of State Thomas Jefferson.

Secretary Hamilton believed the federal government should pay the states' war debts. He created a financial plan to pay them as well as the national debt. Hamilton also successfully created a Bank of the United States, despite the opposition of southerners like Madison and Jefferson.

Alexander Hamilton (pictured) became part of the first presidential Cabinet when he served as Secretary of the Treasury under President George Washington.

Hamilton's financial plan and the success of a national bank helped ensure the new nation's financial future. He left the Treasury in January 1795.

Hamilton found himself out of step with his fellow Federalists and scorned by the Democratic-Republicans. A small scandal, involving an extramarital affair, in addition to the death of his son, forced Hamilton to resign from public office. He was in a deep depression that lasted many months.

Whether he worked behind the political scenes in support of the passage of the Constitution or for the elections of Washington and Jefferson, Hamilton was usually successful. In 1804 Hamilton opposed Republican party leader and Vice-President Aaron Burr in his bid to be governor of New York. Despite his diminishing political power, Hamilton again was successful. Burr took Hamilton's opposition as a personal insult and challenged him to a duel. Duels were a common way for men in the eighteenth and early nineteenth centuries to settle their differences.

Hamilton's son Phillip had been killed in a duel in 1801. Hamilton had advised him that a Christian man shouldn't shoot another man in a duel.

Hamilton's strong sense of honor compelled him to attend his own duel. History couldn't record what he was thinking as he stood in a Weehawken, New Jersey, field on July 11, 1804. However, Hamilton remained true to his beliefs and didn't fire his pistol. Burr shot him.

In the hours after the he was shot, his wife—who would survive him by fifty years—visited Hamilton with their seven children. He died in the afternoon of July 12, 1804, with Gouverneur Morris by his side. Hamilton, ever the efficient clerk, had left a complete will and arranged his business affairs before the duel.

Hamilton's political theories are widely discussed and often applied to today's political problems. His great contribution to the new country and to the importance of the national Treasury is memorialized on the ten-dollar bill.

3

John Jay

Reluctant Revolutionary

Just as John Adams never strayed from his strong Puritan upbringing, John Jay always remained close to his French Huguenot roots. He never forgot that his ancestors in Europe had been persecuted for their religious beliefs. Because of this persecution, they had emigrated to the New World in search of religious freedom.

John was born on December 12, 1745, to a wealthy New York City merchant. As a result, he always associated with society's upper class.

John was a bright and quick student. In 1760, when he was only fourteen years old, he entered King's College in New York City. After college Jay served as a lawyer's apprentice for five years and studied law.

John Jay

Jay quickly established himself as a talented lawyer. Several times he argued cases against fellow King's College graduate Gouverneur Morris, with whom he had a long and deep friendship.

Jay first entered public life in July 1769. He served as the clerk of the royal commission responsible for determining the boundary between New York and New Jersey.

On April 28, 1774, Jay married Sarah Van Brugh Livingston, a daughter of William Livingston. Livingston would serve as the wartime governor of New Jersey and would sign the Constitution. Sally, as she was called, was charming, outgoing, beautiful, and eleven years younger than Jay. A popular and stylish hostess, she complemented her husband's often reserved personality.

They were married for more than thirty years and were seldom separated. Sally even accompanied her husband overseas on a diplomatic mission during the Revolutionary War. Jay's family responsibilities extended beyond Sally. At one point in his life, Jay was financially responsible for seven people. Without complaining and with unwavering generosity, he supported his elderly mother and father and his older sister, Eve, whose husband had left her. Jay also supported and raised Eve's son, Peter Jay Munro. He also provided for his older brother, Augustus, who was mentally handicapped and could not read or write. His brother Peter and his sister Anna, who were both left blind after the smallpox epidemic of 1739, also benefited from Jay's generosity.[1]

A devoutly religious man himself, Jay respected the rights of people who held different religious beliefs. When the Continental Congress first met in September 1774, twenty-nine-year-old Jay opposed opening the government's business day with a prayer. He recognized that people worshiped differently.[2]

Although he was tolerant of different beliefs, he held negative feelings toward those of the Catholic faith. Jay's ancestors had been persecuted in Europe by Catholics. Jay felt that Catholics would be loyal to priests and the pope rather than state authority. His multiple attempts to discriminate against Catholics in the new New York State Constitution were opposed by his old friend Gouverneur Morris.

By September 1774, political feelings toward colonial independence were changing. For the first time, the thirteen colonies were speaking with one voice, but the message usually was debated long and hard. Jay was one of the more moderate members of the Continental Congress. He often found himself opposed by the more radical founding father, Richard Henry Lee.

Jay and Lee served on a committee responsible for drafting a letter to their fellow British subjects explaining the position of the colonists. Lee's draft was far too radical and was received with dead silence.[3] Another member of the committee suggested Jay's version of the letter. In October,

Congress adopted Jay's "Address to the People of Great Britain." It was quickly approved and distributed worldwide.

With the publication of his letter, Jay quickly earned a reputation as a leader all over the colonies. But when the Second Continental Congress met in 1775, Jay, like most other colonists, still supported a reconciliation with Great Britain.

Jay continued to oppose radicals and the independence movement. But as events unfolded and lines were drawn, Jay found himself embracing their cause. In November 1775, Jay asked for and received a commission in the New York City militia. He was also elected to the Congress' Committee of Secret Correspondence, which would later become the Committee of Foreign Affairs.

Like many of the other founding fathers, Jay's loyalties were to his family and state before the country. So in the spring and summer of 1776, he remained in New York, a delegate to the New York Provincial Congress. One of the finest legal minds in New York, Jay helped draft the New York State Constitution. That document would later serve as a model for the United States Constitution.

A highly principled man, Jay was usually very cautious and always followed established procedures. But once Congress committed to revolution, Jay became a leading supporter. He drafted New York's resolution supporting the Declaration of Independence and organized a network of informants to spy on the British. Jay once suggested that New York City be burned to prevent the British from using the thriving port city as an important base of operations.

As Jay's reputation as a statesman and legal scholar grew, he faced more and more demands on his time. He proved to be so popular that December 1778 found him in three major offices. He served as a member of the New York delegation to the Continental Congress. He also was the first chief justice of the New York Supreme Court, to which he'd been elected in May 1777. And he was the newly elected president of the Continental Congress.

Jay served as Congress president for nearly ten months and resigned when he was named the minister to Spain. At the end of the war, Jay, along with John Adams, was one of the commissioners who negotiated peace with Great Britain. Jay signed the Treaty of Paris on September 3, 1783.

Jay returned to New York in July 1784, to find that the Congress had elected him the new secretary for foreign affairs. As secretary, Jay represented a weak and powerless national government. The government lacked the power to collect taxes or to force states to deliver their obligations. He came to recognize the obvious shortcomings of the existing Articles of Confederation and continued to support a strong central government. "I have long thought," Jay wrote to Thomas Jefferson in 1786, and become daily more convinced that the construction of our Federal government is fundamentally wrong. To vest legislative, judicial, and executive powers in one and the same body of men and that, too, in a body daily changing its members, can never be wise. In my opinion, these three great departments of sovereignty should be forever separated, and so distributed as to serve as checks on each other.[4]

Jay didn't participate in the Constitutional Convention of 1787, but he did support the Federalist movement behind the new document. Along with founding fathers Alexander Hamilton and James Madison, Jay helped write the *The Federalist* papers, published in support of the Constitution. He wrote five of the eighty-five essays before illness forced him to stop.

When the new form of government was adopted, Jay was named the first Chief Justice of the Supreme Court. He served from 1789 to 1795. In 1794, he traveled to England on official business without his beloved Sally. While apart for twelve months, they wrote to each other three times a week and numbered their letters in case they were delivered out of order.[5] While in England Jay settled remaining disagreements between the two countries. As President Washington's special emissary, Jay negotiated what became known as Jay's Treaty. The agreement settled some issues, and ended British occupation of the western frontier. However, Jay and Washington were

In 1789, Jay became the first Chief Justice of the Supreme Court.

criticized for giving the British too much. The new nation was economically and militarily weak, and the treaty was the best the United States could hope for. The Senate eventually ratified the treaty.

Jay was nominated as governor of New York State while he was still in England. He was elected within days of his return. In June 1795, Jay was inaugurated governor, two days after resigning as Chief Justice of the U.S. Supreme Court.

Governor Jay reformed New York in many ways. He improved the treatment of prisoners and managed state finances better. Through a friend in the legislature, he worked to end slavery in the state. Jay served as governor for two terms until 1801.

As Jay prepared to step down from the governor's office and retire forever from public life, he received a letter from President John Adams. The president told Jay that he had been appointed a second time as Chief Justice of the Supreme Court. In his late fifties, Jay wasn't interested in riding from federal circuit court to circuit court, and he declined his old seat.

After a long life dedicated to public service, Jay retired to Bedford, New York. In his final years, until his death in May 1829, Jay dedicated his time to the religious devotion that had sustained him all his life.

Thomas Jefferson

4

Thomas Jefferson
Architect of Democracy

Thomas Jefferson, like John Jay, was born into one of the top social circles. He dedicated his public life to helping others better their lives.

Jefferson was born at Shadwell plantation in the Blue Ridge Mountains on April 13, 1743. He came from one of the more influential families in western Virginia. His father, Peter Jefferson, was a wealthy and successful planter and mapmaker. His mother, Jane Randolph, was from one of Virginia's most prominent families. Peter died when Thomas was fourteen, leaving him the heir to a massive estate.

The elder Jefferson had insisted that his oldest son receive the formal education he never had. Tall and shy, the bookish sixteen-year-old Thomas entered the College of William and Mary in

Williamsburg, Virginia, in the spring of 1760. After graduating two years later, Jefferson stayed in Virginia's capital city and studied law.

As a lawyer, Jefferson specialized in registering, transferring, and reregistering land deeds for wealthy landowners. His successes increased both his and his clients' wealth.

On January 1, 1772, Jefferson married twenty-three-year-old Martha Skelton Wayles. Together in their mountain home, Monticello, they had six children. Only two daughters, Martha and Mary, survived to adulthood.

"I am as happy nowhere else, . . . and all my wishes end, where I hope my days will, at Monticello," Jefferson said of his beloved home.[1] He spent his life tearing down, redesigning, and adding to the building. Historian Arthur Schlesinger, Jr., called Monticello "the most civilized house in American history."[2]

Jefferson was elected to Virginia's House of Burgesses in 1769. In his autobiography he wrote that he served for several years with "Nothing of particular excitement occurring for a considerable time."[3]

After arranging communication between the individual colonial governments, Jefferson represented Virginia at the Second Continental Congress in 1775. Jefferson was known for his writing ability, though he very seldom spoke. "During the whole Time I satt [sic] with him in Congress," John Adams wrote, "I never heard him utter three Sentences together."[4]

The next year, Jefferson was named to a committee—which included founding fathers John Adams and Roger Sherman—to draft the Declaration of Independence. Jefferson asked Adams to write the important document, but the committee wanted the author to be a Southerner and a Virginian. A southern author would demonstrate the strong support for independence outside Massachusetts and Pennsylvania. Adams insisted that Jefferson write it. As he recalled years later, he told Jefferson: "Reason first—You are a Virginian, and a Virginian ought to appear at the head of this business. Reason second— I am so obnoxious and unpopular. You are very much otherwise. Reason third—You can write ten times better than I can."[5]

Jefferson drew on several great political philosophers for ideas. In the Declaration of Independence, Jefferson outlined and defined basic American liberties. These liberties would come to be considered a standard for most civilized countries in the world. All people are equal and entitled to basic human rights and liberties, the Declaration said, and not just those born to certain social or economic groups.

While serving in the Continental Congress, Jefferson also was reelected to the state legislature. Thinking he could be of better use in Virginia, Jefferson resigned from Congress. After spending a short time with his sick wife, Jefferson took his place in the state legislature in October 1776. For the next two years, Jefferson helped rewrite

Jefferson was known for his writing ability. His greatest work, the Declaration of Independence, established the United States of America as a new country.

many of Virginia's laws. His most significant accomplishments were designed to help talented individuals who were not born to high social standing. The "Bill for Establishing Religious Freedom" passed some years later, but his "Bill for the More General Diffusion of Knowledge" never became law.

In 1779, Jefferson moved from the legislature to the governor's mansion while the Revolutionary War raged. Jefferson was a leading political thinker and a skilled lawyer, but he had no military experience. Also, he headed a weak state government with no army to defend it. The reserved Virginian resigned the governor's office after two years and returned to Monticello and his family.

In the quiet of his mountain home, Jefferson was finally free to pursue his interests and desires. An accomplished violinist, Jefferson often played with his daughters and for visitors. Music touched Jefferson so deeply that he often quietly and unconsciously hummed under his breath.[6]

Jefferson's wife suffered ill health for most of their marriage, and the demands at home often pulled him away from his public commitments. Martha grew sicker and eventually died on September 6, 1782, with her husband at her side. For the last forty-four years of his life, Jefferson kept his promise to her that he would never remarry. In the days after her death, Jefferson destroyed all their letters to each other and nearly all her belongings. Many think he burned the letters because of his grief. Others theorize that he destroyed them because of his highly private nature.

In March 1785, Jefferson became minister to France. Along with Adams, Jefferson was responsible for negotiating trade treaties. While in Europe Jefferson shipped crates of books back to his friend James Madison, and bought china and mirrors for Abigail Adams. He spent huge sums expanding his own library, wine cellar, and collections of furniture and art. In France, Jefferson established spending patterns that would eventually lead him down a dark road of debt.

When Jefferson returned in 1789, he learned that he was appointed the new country's first secretary of state. Serving through 1793, Jefferson was a trusted advisor to President Washington. As a small-government advocate, Jefferson often disagreed with the expansive views of Treasury Secretary Alexander Hamilton.

Jefferson spent three years at his beloved Monticello before reentering public life in 1796. Jefferson was the Democratic-Republican party's candidate for president against John Adams's Federalist party. Jefferson helped form the Democratic-Republican party because he was not happy with the far-reaching nationalist actions of Hamilton and Adams.

Jefferson lost to Adams by three electoral votes and became vice-president. After being sworn in, the quiet, unassuming Jefferson returned to his boarding-house and had a quiet dinner with his fellow lodgers.

In 1800, Adams and Jefferson ran against each other again, and this time Jefferson won. His election marked the first transfer of power from one political party to another. As the leader of his party, Jefferson kept firm control over congressional Republicans.

With Jefferson, the presidency grew less formal than it had been under former general George Washington and Puritan John Adams. Jefferson could often be seen riding around the capital on horseback rather than in a carriage. He held cabinet meetings at a round table so no one person sat at the table's head.

Jefferson was less formal, with one major exception. Washington and Adams both delivered their State of the Union addresses to Congress personally. Jefferson had the House and Senate clerks read the annual presidential messages. This tradition stood for more than one hundred years. He so disliked public speaking that his inaugural addresses were his only two public speeches in eight years in the White House.[7]

The low point in Jefferson's career occurred in 1802. Federalist newspapers circulated negative rumors about Jefferson's private life. He refused to address the rumors publicly.

Jefferson achieved the high point of his presidency in 1803 with the Louisiana Purchase. Jefferson purchased from the French the land rights to the western part of the continent. The cost was about three cents an acre, or around $15 million. This more than doubled the size of the new nation. Despite the controversial rumors started a few years before, Jefferson was easily reelected in 1804.

His second term was made difficult with the growing tensions in Europe and the financial troubles created by the Embargo Act of 1807. This act limited importation and exportation of goods. At the end of his second term in 1809, Jefferson left the White House and returned to Monticello. At sixty-five he retired from politics, but not from public life.

In 1815, Jefferson sold more than six thousand of his books to the Library of Congress, which had been burned by the British in the War of 1812. In 1819, he founded the University of Virginia in Charlottesville. He designed the university's curriculum and all the buildings himself.

Jefferson died early on the afternoon of July 4, 1826, only a few hours before John Adams.

Jefferson believed that his greatest accomplishments were the religious and political freedoms he helped secure and the educational opportunities he helped create. Before his death, ever the meticulously planning architect, Jefferson designed his headstone and wrote his own epitaph: "Here was buried Thomas Jefferson; Author of the Declaration of American Independence, of the Statute of Virginia for Religious Freedom & Father of the University of Virginia."[8]

5

Richard Henry Lee
Southern Radical

Richard Henry Lee was born on January 20, 1732, in Westmoreland County, Virginia. He was educated in England and groomed for a refined life of gentility and leadership.

Lee married Anne Aylett in December 1757, when he was twenty-five years old. Over the next few years, two of Lee's brothers married Anne's sister and half sister. The extreme closeness of his family also extended into the political world.

Lee replaced his half brother-in-law in the Virginia House of Burgesses in 1758. Lee's three brothers and two of his first cousins also served in state government that year.

Lee quickly established himself as a strong public speaker when he attacked the leader of the House for

Richard Henry Lee

having too much power. His public opposition to the unpopular Stamp Act, passed in England by the House of Commons, added to his political reputation.

His growing reputation kept up with his growing family. Lee's first son was born in October 1758. Two years later his second son was born. In 1764, Anne gave birth to their first daughter. A second daughter was born in 1766.

Success in business and triumphs in politics were soon overshadowed by tragedy at home. One day Lee's gun exploded in a hunting accident, badly maiming his left hand. His months of recuperation kept him at home. He was unable to publicly oppose the latest group of taxes imposed on the colonies by England. In December 1768, Anne and their two sons became gravely ill. The boys recovered, but she did not. With her death, Lee found himself with four children to take care of alone. The following summer he married Anne Gaskins Pinckard. Together he and Anne had three more children.

Over the course of two years, Lee met several times with Thomas Jefferson and Virginia's other young elected leaders in the public rooms of Williamsburg taverns. The two tall, thin redheads agreed that each colony should establish a Committee of Correspondence to communicate with each other. They also proposed a meeting of delegates from each colony. This was the first step in uniting the individual colonies.

When the First Continental Congress met in Philadelphia in September 1774, Lee was a member of the Virginia delegation. In late October he chaired the committee responsible for drafting an address to the king. The letter outlined the grievances of the colonies.

Congress considered Lee's draft to be too radical and instead approved John Jay's "Address to the People of Great Britain." Lee was often at odds with the conservative members of Congress, including Jay. Jay didn't introduce the letter himself, and many members didn't know he was the author. Lee contributed to the misunderstanding by telling people that Jay's father-in-law wrote the address. Months later, Jay finally confronted Lee in the halls of Congress and, holding him by the button of his coat, sternly reminded him that he was the true author. Thomas Jefferson was drawn into the argument and later wrote that "These gentlemen had had some sparrings in debate before, and continued ever very hostile to each other."[1]

Like Jefferson, Lee traveled between Philadelphia for congressional business and Virginia for state business. Lee represented Westmoreland County at the Virginia Convention of 1775. On March 23, Lee listened as Patrick Henry gave his famous "Give me liberty or give me death" speech. Along with fellow delegate Jefferson, Lee rose in support of Henry's resolution to raise and arm a state militia.

Richard Henry Lee (pictured), a Virginian radical, was often at odds with conservative New Yorker John Jay.

As war with Great Britain seemed increasingly probable, Lee led Virginia to the front of the independence movement. Lee returned to the Second Continental Congress in the spring of 1775. Although violence had not yet found its way to Virginia, British troops had exchanged shots with Massachusetts citizens at Lexington and Concord. Lee's work in Congress that year was impressive. He served on six of the nine committees and chaired three of them.

When the Continental Congress met in the spring of 1776, Lee planned to change the ongoing negotiations with Great Britain. Lee knew that alliances between the united colonies and other world powers were necessary to prevent Great Britain from crushing the rebellion and dividing the colonies.

As the spring weather warmed, so too did Lee's quest for independence. He formed an alliance with founding father John Adams and the Massachusetts delegation. Lee and Adams encouraged other delegates to consider new forms of state and national governments. The Virginia Convention unanimously passed a resolution supporting independence.

News of the resolution washed over Philadelphia like a wave. Within a few weeks, the time was right for Lee to propose cutting all ties to Great Britain. On Friday June 7, 1776, Lee introduced a resolution that "these United Colonies are, and of right ought to be, free and independent states, that they are absolved from all allegiance to the British Crown and that all political connection between them and the State of Great Britain is, and ought to be, totally dissolved."[2]

Lee introduced the resolution for independence. But the Virginia delegation appointed thirty-three-year-old Thomas Jefferson to the committee charged with drafting the Declaration of Independence. In his autobiography years later, John Adams wrote that "Mr. Richard Henry Lee was not beloved by the most of his Colleagues from Virginia and Mr. Jefferson was sett up to rival and supplant him."[3]

In fact, when the committee was appointed on June 11, Lee had already made plans to return to Virginia. On June 13, Lee left for Williamsburg to help create the new state government. Lee arrived in time to vote on the new state constitution and the Declaration of Rights written by George Mason.

Over the summer of 1776, Lee received several letters from Jefferson in Philadelphia. Jefferson wanted to return to his sick wife at Monticello, so he repeatedly begged Lee to take his place in the Continental Congress. Lee returned to Congress in late August and got right back to work. In the next three months he served on eighteen different committees.

But in May 1777, Adams's description of Lee and his fellow Virginians proved to be grounded in truth. Virginians failed to reelect Lee to Congress. There were rumors that Lee was not interested in his state's concerns. Lee defended his actions and saved his reputation. He returned to Congress in August 1777, where he continued to support a united government for the colonies.

Illness forced Lee to leave Congress in December, and he didn't return until the following May. Lee served on more than fifty special committees in a six-month period. His dedication to his job strained his health, and he finally resigned in May 1779.

Away from Congress, Lee turned his attention to the needs of his state. As a colonel in the militia, Lee led troops against the British near his native Westmoreland County. Lee returned to Virginia's House of Delegates in 1780, although he was too ill to attend several sessions.

In 1784, Lee again was elected to the Congress. The man who had once been a leading Congressional radical and had been one of the first to call for independence was unanimously elected the president of Congress. Lee served for the one-year term before returning home to rest.

Lee was appointed to the Constitutional Convention of 1787. Publicly, Lee declined the appointment because of his poor health. Privately, Lee thought it was wrong for him to work on the Constitution that he would eventually have to approve as a member of Congress.[4] In the days before the convention, he wrote a long letter to George

Mason, outlining his views of the future of the federal government.

When the new Constitution was delivered in the fall, Lee was surprised by the convention members' ambitious attempt to redesign government. He demanded that approval be debated and not rashly rushed. He supported many amendments and changes to the proposed document, including a Bill of Rights. Lee tried to stop what he believed were attacks against the rights of the states and individuals. Although he didn't participate in the ratification convention, Lee was disappointed when Virginia approved the Constitution without requiring amendments but only recommending them.

After the first Congressional election in 1788, the presidency, the House of Representatives, and the Senate all were filled with supporters of a strong national government. Lee and his fellow senator from Virginia, William Grayson, were the only anti-Federalists in the Senate.

Lee served on several committees in the Senate and continued to call for a Bill of Rights and amendments to the Constitution. He saw the first ten amendments pass successfully, but poor health frequently kept him out of the Senate. However, his dedication to the new nation was recognized when the Senate elected him president pro tempore. He presided temporarily over the Senate in the absence of the vice-president. Lee served for a little less than a month before the session ended, and he returned home for the final time.

Ever dedicated to the public good, Lee wrote to President George Washington, just a month before he died on June 19, 1794. In this last letter, Lee shared with his old friend his opinion on such important issues as commerce, foreign affairs, and the threat of war. He reminded Washington that like all the other founding fathers, they shared the same basic goals and that "the Success & happiness of the United States is our care."[5]

6

James Madison

Father of the Constitution

James Madison was born March 5, 1751, at Port Conway, Virginia, the home of his maternal grandfather. He grew up on the family estate, Montpelier, where he lived for most of his life. A frail child, James was sickly nearly all his life. He was such a hypochondriac that he was afraid to travel or exert himself.

His father was a very wealthy planter and slaveholder. Like many other of his fellow founding fathers, James never had to worry about earning a living. He studied law, religion, and political theory, and he had read every book in Montpelier by the time he was eleven.

Because Madison was held back due to his frailty, he was several years older than most of his classmates

James Madison

when he entered the College of New Jersey (now Princeton University). He completed three years worth of courses in two years and graduated in September 1771. Concerns for his health forced him to cut short graduate studies in ethics, Hebrew, and theology. In 1772 he returned home, where he tutored his seven younger brothers and sisters.

As the colonies moved closer to war with England, the sickly Madison was sure he would not play a part. He wrote to a friend that he was "too dull and infirm now to look out for extraordinary things in this world, but my sensations for many months have intimated to me not to expect a long or healthy life."[1]

Despite his real and imagined infirmities, Madison took his first step into the public spotlight in December 1774. He was elected to the Orange County Committee of Safety, the local governing body. Although he was warm and funny when talking with close friends, Madison was quiet around strangers.

His shyness did not prevent his fellow Virginians from electing him to the Virginia Convention in 1776. He was also elected to the General Assembly, where he served alongside George Mason, Richard Henry Lee, and Thomas Jefferson.

Like Jefferson, Madison was soft-spoken. But the two were strikingly different physically. The five-and-a-half-feet-tall Madison looked up to the six-feet-two-inch Jefferson in many ways. Madison and Jefferson shared many political views and quickly became lifelong friends and allies. Madison, Jefferson wrote later, was a fine politician "soothing always the feelings of his adversaries by civilities and softness of expression."[2]

From January 1778 to December 1779, Madison served on Virginia's Council of State under governors Thomas Jefferson and Patrick Henry. Madison served for several years in the Continental Congress before returning to the Virginia General Assembly in 1784. In the General Assembly he worked for passage of Jefferson's Statute for Religious Freedom. Madison joined Jefferson to oppose the government's support of religion, first in Virginia and then at the national level. Madison helped build what Jefferson called the "wall of separation" between church and state.

At the Annapolis Convention in 1786, Madison and George Washington helped settle a dispute between Virginia and Maryland over navigational rights of the Potomac River.

After the Annapolis Convention, delegates traveled to the National Convention of 1787 to discuss trade and other important issues. They knew the Articles of Confederation would probably be changed in some way. But few delegates were as willing as Madison to completely scrap the existing form of government and go in an entirely new direction.

When Madison rode into Philadelphia that spring, he brought with him his plan for the future of the nation. Submitted on May 29, the plan came to be called the Virginia Plan. Madison proposed a strong federal government divided into legislative, executive, and judicial branches. Under the plan, the federal government would be more powerful than the weakened state governments.

Madison had perfect attendance at the convention and took extensive notes. Today his notes give historians the most complete picture of how our form of government came to be. Between his note taking and his drafting of legislation, Madison still found time to speak at the convention 161 times. Only two other delegates spoke more often than he.

His many contributions to the completed Constitution were only half the battle. Madison knew that there would be no new nation if the states didn't ratify the Constitution.

Madison joined with fellow Federalists Alexander Hamilton and John Jay in writing *The Federalist* papers. Hamilton's essays often discussed the future possibilities of the fledgling nation. Madison reflected the beliefs of his fellow Virginians in many of his twenty-eight essays. He wrote about the necessary limits of government. Hamilton and Madison both supported a strong national government uninfluenced by the daily emotions and pressures of the common people.

Madison knew that the population of the new nation would grow. He knew that the problems facing the million colonists in the late 1700s wouldn't be the same problems facing future Americans. And he knew the new Constitution would serve all Americans—present and future. Madison left Hamilton and New York in time to serve in Virginia's ratification convention in June 1788.

Madison debated each point of the Constitution with founding father and anti-Federalist George Mason, who refused to sign the document in Philadelphia. Madison became ill during the debates. He allowed other Federalists to voice their support and debate other conservative Virginians.

Virginia eventually adopted the Constitution. But much to his disappointment, Madison's anti-Federalist opponents in the General Assembly prevented his election to the new United States Senate.

His friends back in Orange County elected him to the United States House of Representatives, where he continued building and strengthening the new government. In Congress, Madison took personal control of the first proposed amendments. Many feared that the anti-Federalists would weaken the government he had worked so hard to create.

The passage of the Bill of Rights, the first ten amendments to the Constitution, was the most significant event of the first year of Congress. The Bill of Rights may even be the most important group of laws Congress has ever passed.

During his four terms in the House of Representatives, Madison opposed Hamilton's plan for the federal government to pay state war debts. He also helped Jefferson found the Democratic-Republican party. Madison demonstrated that he supported a federal government with limited powers and control.

In September 1794, Madison married Dolley Payne Todd. After stepping down from the House of Representatives in March 1797, Madison retired to Montpelier. Back home, Madison enjoyed married life and entertained guests. His old friend Thomas Jefferson would stop by on his way to and from the national capital in New York.

Madison again took to the national stage in May 1801, when he served as Jefferson's secretary of state. Secretary Madison supervised the Louisiana Purchase of 1803. He also helped create the Embargo Act of 1807. The Embargo Act was Jefferson's response to the growing threat of war with England or France, who were still hostile to each other. The act prohibited United States merchants from exporting or importing goods and subsequently damaged American commerce.

Madison inherited all the problems associated with the Embargo Act when he became the fourth president of United States in March 1809. Although the Embargo Act expired the day before he took office, the success of United States trade remained clouded for years. The United States had no real navy or world-class army. It had no realistic way to stop British and French ships from boarding and seizing

In 1809, Madison became the fourth president of the United States.

United States trade ships anywhere in the world. Madison also allowed the charter of the Bank of the United States to expire. This jeopardized the nation's future economic well-being.

Finally, in June 1812, President Madison extinguished all avenues of diplomacy with Great Britain. For the first time, the United States of America declared war on another nation. Madison's war lasted nearly three years and moved slowly until August 1814, when British forces invaded and burned Washington, D.C. The sixty-three-year-old Madison personally supervised the evacuation of the capital city from horseback.

In January 1815, the war ended with a peace treaty. A new national commitment was made to the union that Madison had worked so hard to create and maintain.

Madison finally left public life and retired to Montpelier in April 1817. In his retirement he edited and published the notes he had taken during the Constitutional Convention of 1787.

Despite his infirmities, including bad teeth that caused him great pain, Madison lived to age eighty-five. He died on June 28, 1836, having survived every other signer of the Constitution.

George Mason

7

George Mason

Father of Virginia's Declaration of Rights

With a heart dedicated to his native Virginia, George Mason spoke out above all others at the Constitutional Convention in 1787. He loudly and repeatedly opposed the emerging new form of government.

Born December 11, 1725, in Fairfax County, Virginia, George Mason was the fourth of a long line of George Masons. Through business or marriage, George was connected to most of the important families in the colony. Educated at home by his mother and private tutors, George enjoyed learning. He eventually became one of Virginia's most learned leaders.

When George was ten years old, his father drowned during a storm. George then became the heir to family estates and lands in Virginia and Maryland.

The adult Mason recognized his standing in society. Although he didn't enjoy holding elected office and being in the public eye, he understood the civic responsibilities of a gentleman. He dutifully accepted the positions to which he was elected.[1]

The year 1749 found Mason assuming some of his first public responsibilities and looking to expand his financial fortunes. He became a justice of the Fairfax County Court and was elected to an important leadership position in the church. He invested in land and would eventually own tens of thousands of acres of land in western Virginia.

In April 1750, Mason married Ann Eilbeck. Ann's important family connections in Maryland furthered Mason's growing business interests.

In 1755, Mason began construction of Gunston Hall. The huge building was completed in 1758, and it remained Mason's home for the rest of his life. Mason ran the daily operations of his plantation by himself, without the assistance of a manager or overseer. That same year, Mason was elected to the Virginia House of Burgesses, where he served until 1761. At around the same time, Mason attained the rank of colonel while serving as a quartermaster during the French and Indian War.

In the years after the war, Great Britain tried to pay off its war debts by passing laws and taxes that applied only to British subjects living in the

American colonies. Like many of the other colonists in the 1760s and early 1770s, Mason was still loyal to the king. Despite his loyalty, Mason believed these acts interfered with the rights of people living in the colonies. In his Fairfax Resolves of July 1774, Mason moved to the front of the independence movement. He announced Fairfax County's demand for additional rights and freedoms. Later, Virginia colonists would make the same demand.

Mason cherished his time away from the public eye. But from Gunston Hall, he kept involved in the independence movement by corresponding with other colonial leaders. His days as a private citizen ended in 1775 when he replaced his neighbor George Washington as the Fairfax County representative to the state government. When the royal governor fled Virginia shortly before the revolution, Mason was elected to the Committee of Safety. This committee took the governor's place as the leader of the state.

The next year, Mason helped write Virginia's new state constitution. He also made his greatest contribution to the rights of Virginians and all other colonists. His contribution would eventually affect nearly every person in the world. Virginia's Declaration of Rights was part of the state's new constitution. Mason wrote "Virginia's Bill of Rights" in less than a month. For the first time in political history, someone wrote down what today are considered the basic rights of humanity. Virginia's Declaration of Rights passed unanimously on June 12, 1776.

The free exercise of religion, freedom of the press, and many other rights of the individual were now the new laws of Virginia. While these basic rights were adopted and respected, it was still necessary to ensure that old state laws reflected the new rights. Mason served on a commission charged with revising state laws. He also worked to preserve and protect the rights of the individual.

Between January 1777 and January 1779, Mason worked closely with founding father Thomas Jefferson. Mason was "a man of the first order of wisdom among those who acted on the theatre of the revolution, of expansive mind, profound judgement, . . ." Jefferson said of his fellow Virginian. "His language was strong, his manner most impressive, and strengthened by a dash of biting cynicism, when provocation made it seasonable."[2]

In May 1777, Mason was elected to Congress. He declined the position. Like Jefferson, he chose to continue his work on the new state government. As he strengthened his state's government, Mason soon saw the weaknesses in the national government. Mason traveled to Philadelphia and the Constitutional Convention of 1787 in support of a new government. Once he arrived in Philadelphia, Mason didn't like the suggestions he heard for weakening the rights of the states.

A vocal member of the convention, Mason spoke 136 times during the debates. His fellow delegates often got a taste of his "biting cynicism" when day after day he rose to argue against proposed elements of the new document. Mason deeply believed that the deals that were struck would forever change the nature of government. He thought that the agreements would negatively affect that which he prized above all else—the rights of the individuals.

Mason opposed the idea of a strong president. He was against using the power of the federal government to tax goods shipped across state lines. He also wanted the new government to end the slave trade.

Though Mason opposed slavery, he owned three hundred slaves. Like many other Southerners who opposed slavery, Mason was caught between morality and economics. Laws in slave states like Virginia made it difficult to free slaves. A judge had to approve before a slave could be freed. Large-scale declarations of freedom were very costly and very rare. Had Mason given his slaves their freedom, he would have had to pay for labor that previously had been free. His costs would have increased, and he wouldn't have been able to compete with other plantations that used slave labor. Freeing his slaves would have ruined Mason financially.

On September 12, founding father Gouverneur Morris and the convention's Committee of Style returned the finished draft of the Constitution. Mason suggested that the plan be "prefaced with a

Mason felt that the United States Constitution should guarantee the rights of individuals.

Bill of Rights" and that "with the aid of the state declarations, a bill might be prepared in a few hours."[3] Mason knew that his own Declaration of Rights would serve the need perfectly. After that long, hot summer his fellow delegates weren't up to the challenge of debating a new list of rights, and every state voted against it.

Mason maintained a perfect attendance record at the convention. On the morning of September 17, he watched as all but two of his fellow delegates in attendance signed the Constitution. More than a dozen delegates had left the convention in the preceding months, and they didn't return to sign the Constitution. Some delegates had personal business to attend to. Some didn't think the convention was important enough to deserve their attention. A few others were like Mason and disagreed with the final document. Mason told his fellow delegates that he couldn't sign a document in Philadelphia that he wouldn't support in Virginia. Days earlier, he told them that he "would sooner chop off his right hand than put it to the Constitution as it now stands."[4]

When the state convention came months later, true to his word, Mason led the debate against the Constitution. After Virginia approved the Constitution, Mason continued to demand a Bill of Rights to protect individuals and the states against the federal government. Although Mason was again a private citizen, he urged fellow Virginian James

Madison to go to Congress in 1789 with a list of proposed amendments.

Mason's reluctance to serve in public office surfaced again in 1790, when the governor of Virginia offered Mason an appointment to the United States Senate. Mason refused to accept the appointment. He was one of only ten surviving members of the Constitutional Convention not to serve in the new government of the United States.

Even after his death, on October 7, 1792, Mason urged his sons to avoid a life of public service. He wrote in his will, "I recommend it to my sons, from my own experience in life, to prefer the happiness of independence and a private station to the troubles and vexations of public business."[5]

Mason didn't contribute many years of his life towards the building of the new nation. He did, however, leave behind one of the most important documents ever written in the name of freedom and liberty.

Mason's Virginia's Declaration of Rights served as the foundation upon which the United States was built. Its influence can be found in the Declaration of Independence. It is the cornerstone of the Constitution's Bill of Rights, ratified on December 15, 1791, and the French Declaration of the Rights of Man and Citizen of 1789. Over a century later, it influenced the United Nations' Universal Declaration of Human Rights of 1949.

8

Gouverneur Morris

Penman of the Constitution

Like so many of the other founding fathers, Gouverneur Morris was born into a well-established and well-to-do family. While he was drawn to public service, Morris also found time to have fun and enjoy life.

Morris was born at the family home in Morrisania, New York, on January 31, 1752. The fourth son in the family, Gouverneur was ten years old when his father died, leaving him a modest inheritance. Following his father's final wishes, Morris attended college. He graduated from King's College when he was sixteen. The quick-witted and likable Morris studied law for three years. The same year he became a lawyer, nineteen-year-old Morris began exchanging letters with fifteen-year-old Sally

Gouverneur Morris

Livingston. Sally was the future bride of his friend, founding father John Jay.

The lighthearted and fun-loving Morris enjoyed the company of women all his life. He was never restrained by religious conservatism, like John Adams, or by bashfulness, like James Madison. He enjoyed life to the fullest in every way.

Standing more than six feet tall, Morris was solidly built and athletic. He lost a leg in an accident at the age of twenty-eight. But the active Morris strapped on a wooden leg and continued to hunt, fish, and enjoy the outdoors.

At only twenty-three years old, Morris entered politics in the spring of 1775. He served in the state government, the New York Provincial Congress. The next year, Morris helped write the state's new constitution. He was joined by his friend, thirty-one-year-old John Jay.

The young Morris proved to be one of the more progressive thinkers in the colonies. He repeatedly opposed the efforts of his friend Jay to create laws that would have discriminated against Catholics. Morris also proposed an amendment that would have abolished slavery in New York. He was able to protect the religious freedoms of all New Yorkers, but his antislavery legislation failed. Despite his efforts, slavery continued in New York for several more years.

Morris's older half brother, Lewis, also was drawn to public service, serving in both Congress and the state government. While Gouverneur worked on the new state constitution, Lewis Morris was in Philadelphia, where he signed the Declaration of Independence. In the spring of 1777, Morris was elected to the Continental Congress.

Morris's native New York served as the principal battleground during the war because of its location in the center of the colonies. The dangers of the British army kept Morris away from Congress until 1778.

Morris served on several leading committees and became an outspoken supporter of General George Washington and his army. Morris traveled with the army on Congress's behalf and exchanged coded letters with John Jay. The two sent coded letters to each other for the rest of their lives.

While prominent men like Thomas Jefferson and John Adams were in their home states or overseas, Morris became a leader in Congress. He was well respected despite his young age and often lighthearted spirit. He wrote a wide variety of documents, including the plans for the final peace with England.

In May 1779, the twenty-six-year-old Morris failed to win reelection and suddenly found himself out of office. The family home in Morrisania was behind enemy lines, so Morris moved to Philadelphia. He practiced law and wrote his "Observations on the American Revolution." Morris spent many months recovering from the riding accident that cost him his left leg. In 1781, after he recovered, he took the position of assistant superintendent of finance, which he held until 1785.

Along with Finance Superintendent Robert Morris—who was no relation—he helped handle the finances of the new confederation. With several suggestions from Thomas Jefferson, he helped create the current coin decimal system and invented the "cent."

A friend and a Pennsylvanian, Robert Morris helped Gouverneur get elected to the Constitutional Convention as a member of the Pennsylvania delegation. Despite spending several weeks in New York after the death of his mother, Morris was very active at the Convention. He addressed the Convention 173 times, more times than any other delegate.

Morris, like many of the aristocratic founding fathers, didn't trust the general population. The founding fathers supported democracy, but they did not want the average man to have too much control over the daily political activities of the nation. Morris agreed with Hamilton that the president and the Senate should be elected for life. He also supported the idea that the Senate be appointed by the president and serve without pay.

Morris opposed giving political power to poor people, but he was the only delegate to seriously attack slavery and the slave trade. Although several of the ideas that Morris supported were not adopted, the Constitution did reflect many of his deep beliefs.

Despite losing his left leg during a riding accident, Morris continued to pursue many outdoor activities.

On September 8, the Constitution was given to the Committee of Style. Because his fellow delegates trusted his abilities, Morris wrote the language of the final document. Years later Morris wrote to a friend, "That Instrument was written by the Fingers which write this Letter."[1] James Madison, the driving force behind the Constitutional Convention, wrote that in giving Morris the job "a better choice could not have been made."[2] Finally, on September 17, Morris, Madison, and thirty-six other representatives signed the document. Delaware delegate George Read signed the Constitution twice, adding John Dickinson's name in his absence.

Many colonial leaders interacted both professionally and personally. For example, in 1787, Morris traveled to Virginia on personal legal business. While in Richmond, he watched founding fathers Richard Henry Lee and George Mason join with other Virginians to debate the Constitution. Morris reported on the proceedings in letters to Hamilton.

During the first few months of 1789, Morris pursued business interests in France. Morris enjoyed his time in Europe. He pursued friendships with the women of Paris, socialized with the very well to do, and enjoyed meals served at the finest tables.

Morris spent his days writing and making social and business calls. In the evenings he attended parties, plays, and lavish dinners. Morris witnessed the storming of the Bastille that freed the prisoners in the

Paris jail and formally launched the French Revolution.

Morris was often in the company of Minister Thomas Jefferson, and he spent several successful years in Europe. Morris's old friend and the nation's new president, George Washington, named him the minister to France. Several senators didn't want him to represent the United States because of his friendships with the French aristocracy. Others didn't like his casual and lighthearted attitude. "I bear him no ill-will," founding father and Connecticut senator Roger Sherman said, "but with regard to moral character I consider him an irreligious and profane man."[3] Despite these vocal opponents, Morris replaced Jefferson and successfully served as the ambassador from 1792 to 1794. He served during the turmoil and confusion of the French Revolution. Morris stepped down as ambassador and enjoyed traveling around Europe for nearly four more years. He returned to Morrisania in January 1799.

Elected to the United States Senate in 1800 to finish another man's term, Morris supported Jefferson's Louisiana Purchase. He was not reelected in 1802 and retired to the quiet life of Morrisania.

He delivered the eulogies for his old friends George Washington and Alexander Hamilton and succeeded Hamilton as a trustee of Columbia University. Morris also helped pay Hamilton's debts and provided for his family's financial well-being. When he was fifty-seven, Morris finally married

Anne Randolph. Their only child, Gouverneur, was born February 9, 1813. Morris asked his old friend John Jay to be the godfather of his son, but the elderly Jay declined.

Morris never completely retired from public service. The state legislature appointed him chairman of the Erie Canal Commission in 1810. While construction of the important waterway was successful, it would be many years before Morris's idea of building bridges to Manhattan would become a reality.

Morris ended his days at Morrisania, watching his son grow and writing long letters commenting on the political affairs of the day. The man who had pursued personal pleasure while influencing public policy died November 6, 1816.

William Paterson

9

William Paterson

Small States Champion

William Paterson's story began in humble circumstances on the green and rocky fields of Ireland. He was born December 24, 1745, in County Antrim. Paterson then immigrated to North America with his parents, Richard and Mary Paterson, in 1747. He grew up in Princeton, New Jersey. His father, a tinsmith and peddler, ran a shop there. Richard Paterson worked hard so that William could attend private schools before moving on to college.

William could see that most of his classmates had advantages influencing their future success. Unlike them, however, his family didn't have high social standing. William knew that he could only succeed through hard work and a strong education.

Paterson received his bachelor's degree from the College of New Jersey (now Princeton University) in 1763. He earned his master's degree there in 1766. For several years he studied law under Richard Stockton, who would become a signer of the Declaration of Independence. Paterson became a lawyer in 1769. He spent nearly ten years moving between the city and the rural counties, trying to establish his law practice. At one point in the early days of his career, he tried to earn a little more money by running a store with his brother.

In 1775, Paterson was selected as a delegate to the First Provincial Congress of New Jersey. Later that year he served as the secretary of the New Jersey State Congress. Paterson continued to work hard for the people of New Jersey and to advance his growing private legal practice. In 1776, this rural lawyer from humble beginnings was appointed the first attorney general of New Jersey. The honor reflected and rewarded both his ability and his ambition.

After a three-year courtship, Paterson married Cornelia Bell in February 1779. Their first daughter, Cornelia, was born the following year. Their second daughter, Frances, was born in January 1782. Paterson loved his family very much, but his dedication to his work and to the Revolution often kept him away from home.

Paterson strongly supported the independence movement. As attorney general, he actively opposed the Loyalists who stood in the way of independence.

He prosecuted and seized the property of hundreds of people who remained loyal to Great Britain and the king. Paterson also maintained his private practice and found his personal list of clients growing.

In 1778, Paterson was selected to serve in the Continental Congress. He refused the appointment because he was too busy as the state of New Jersey's leading lawyer. He was chosen again in 1781. Again, because of his work—and an unwillingness to leave both his family and his private practice—he refused to serve.

With the war won and the prospect of a prosperous peace on the horizon, the year 1783 held the promise of happy times for Paterson and his family. He planned to step down as attorney general. But the happiness for which he had worked so hard was not to be. In June his youngest child became ill and died. Cornelia, who was pregnant with their third child, became ill with grief. William, their first son, was born in October. Cornelia never recovered from the difficult childbirth, and four days later she died.

Less than two years later, Paterson married Euphemia White, one of Cornelia's closest friends. Paterson was finally living the prestigious life he had admired as a young man. He was recognized and respected in New Jersey's leading circles. After several years out of the public eye, Paterson slowly returned by participating in a regional commission. He also publicly voiced his opinion on the current issues of the day. He commented on the strengths and weaknesses of the Articles of Confederation.

Paterson completed his slow return to public life with his election as the leader of New Jersey's delegation to the Constitutional Convention in 1787. For the Convention's first order of business, the Virginia delegation introduced its plan to consolidate the federal government. The Virginia Plan would have swept aside the equal representation of smaller states under the existing Articles of Confederation. Representatives from the smaller states believed that the larger states were writing a constitution that would forever benefit them at the expense of the small states.

The shortest founding father to attend the Constitutional Convention, Paterson quickly became a leader of the smaller states and represented their interests. On June 15, Paterson submitted his New Jersey Plan. Paterson's plan was little more than a revision of the Articles of Confederation. It was a loose collection of ideas and suggestions proposed as an alternative to the Virginia Plan. The New Jersey Plan called for assigning one vote to each state to protect the independence of the smaller states. Recognizing the importance of a strong justice system, former attorney general Paterson also proposed the creation of a supreme court.

In one of the many compromises at the Constitutional Convention, Paterson's idea was finally applied with the creation of the Senate. In the

Senate each state would be equally represented with two votes. The Great Compromise secured the rights of the smaller states. The number of delegates in the House of Representatives was to be determined by state populations. Satisfied with the compromise, Paterson left the convention in late July.

Like many of the other founding fathers who participated in the Constitutional Convention, Paterson wasn't completely happy with the final document. Despite his minor disagreements, he returned to Philadelphia in September to sign the new Constitution. Also, he supported its adoption at New Jersey's ratifying convention.

New Jersey elected him to the United States Senate that he had helped create when the first Congress met. Paterson served on the Senate's first committee and helped draft the Judiciary Act of 1789. This legislation included sections written in Paterson's own handwriting.

The Judiciary Act created the actual offices of the Supreme Court and established federal district courts in each of the states. These courts would pass judgment over laws of the United States and decide other federal issues.

Remembering his Irish roots, Paterson supported the rights of immigrants. He also favored the financial plan of Treasury Secretary Alexander Hamilton. He supported Hamilton's plan to assume the debts of the states and repay in full national war debts.

In the Senate, Paterson strongly supported the Federalist movement. At the same time, his support back home in New Jersey had never been stronger. Paterson stepped down from the Senate in 1790 to become governor of New Jersey. Paterson had been a well-respected attorney general, and he had successfully defended the rights of New Jersey and the smaller states at the Constitutional Convention. As governor, his popularity reached an all-time high.

That popularity translated into action when Alexander Hamilton came to Paterson with an ambitious plan. Hamilton recognized the endless possibilities available to those who harnessed the power of industry. Hamilton wanted to build the colonial equivalent of an industrial office park on a river shore in New York. Congress refused Hamilton's request for funds for the project, but Paterson supported the idea.

Paterson financed the plan and in 1792 signed the charter of the Society for Establishing Useful Manufactures. The industrial city of Paterson, New Jersey, was founded and named in his honor.

Paterson's four-year Senate term originally was to have ended on March 4, 1793. It was therefore the first day he was eligible to hold another federal office. President Washington appointed him to the United States Supreme Court that same day. By the end of the month, Paterson stepped down as governor and took the oath of a Supreme Court justice.

Paterson became an associate justice of the Supreme Court in 1793.

As an associate justice, Paterson traveled from state to state, riding the circuit of the federal district court system. He used the opportunities to educate local grand juries about the new nation's laws. Paterson worked in his spare time for several years to reform, revise, and rewrite New Jersey's laws, a task he began while serving as governor. He completed the job in 1800 with the "Laws of the State of New Jersey." He continued to serve as an associate justice until his death on September 9, 1806, at his daughter's home in Albany, New York.

From his simple and humble Irish roots to a seat on the United States Supreme Court, William Paterson's life and political career represented the opportunities of the new nation. Paterson demonstrated that through hard work and dedication, he could not only succeed, but also make a special contribution to the pages of history.

Roger Sherman

Witness to History

No other founding father was more involved in nor witnessed more of the birth of the new nation than Roger Sherman.

Sherman was born on April 19, 1721, in Newton, Massachusetts. In 1743, he moved to Connecticut to seek his fortune. Although he had little formal education, like many of the other founding fathers he was eager to learn. At different times in his life Sherman was a cobbler, a merchant, a farmer, a surveyor, and a lawyer.

Sherman was a deeply religious man. His belief in God influenced both his public and his private life. An amateur minister, Sherman wrote and published a book of sermons. He also supported prayers before public meetings.

Roger Sherman

Like other founding fathers, Roger Sherman's natural abilities quickly distinguished him from his neighbors. The shop he ran with his older brother was very successful. In 1745, twenty-four-year-old Sherman first entered public life when he was appointed county surveyor. Three years later, he published an almanac for which he did all the mathematical calculations himself.

The next year, in 1749, Sherman married Elizabeth Hartwell. Together they had seven children. Sherman worked tirelessly to support his growing family. He also supported his widowed mother and two younger brothers. After studying law, he became a lawyer in 1754. Sherman's shift to a career in law changed his life forever, pushing him towards an ever-increasing list of public offices.

No other founding father dedicated his life to public service as deeply as Sherman. Like the others, Sherman was called upon to serve in many different public positions. But unlike most, he often didn't resign from his positions. Sherman was once a judge and a member of the state legislature at the same time. Later in life he served both as a mayor and as a member of Congress.

After only one year of practicing law, Sherman was appointed a justice of the peace for the community of New Milford. Later, he represented the town in the colonial assembly. He returned to the Connecticut Legislature in 1758 and served through

1761. During the same period, Sherman also served as a judge for Litchfield County.

Elizabeth Sherman died in 1760, and the next year Sherman moved to New Haven, Connecticut. His reputation for public service preceded him. Soon Sherman found himself appointed a justice of the peace for New Haven. He represented the town in the colonial assembly for several years. As his public life flourished, Sherman married Rebecca Prescot, with whom he had eight more children.

In 1765, Sherman was again made a judge. Around the same time, he received an appointment as treasurer of Yale University. Yale also awarded him the honorary degree of Master of Arts in 1768. In 1766, he was appointed a judge of the Superior Court of Connecticut, and he was elected to the upper house of the Connecticut general assembly.

Neither Sherman nor the voters of Connecticut saw a conflict with his holding the two positions at once. It was only after nineteen years, in 1785, that he resigned his seat in the upper house. He remained as a Superior Court judge until he was elected to the United States Congress in 1789.

Sherman was still serving as both judge and state assembly representative when he represented Connecticut at the opening session of the First Continental Congress in 1774. The levelheaded intelligence that had been recognized in Connecticut was equally rewarded in Philadelphia. Over the course of several years Sherman's committee work included military matters, trade regulations, and finance. He also served on the committee that drafted the Declaration of Independence.

The next year, Sherman served on the committee appointed to draft the Articles of Confederation. While giving distinguished service to the new national government and protecting the rights of the states, Sherman continued to receive honors back home. During the war he served on the governor's council of safety. In 1783, together with another Superior Court judge, he revised the state laws. In 1784, Sherman was elected the first mayor of New Haven, a position he held for the rest of his life.

Sherman's greatest achievement came three years later. He focused his well-respected insight on a political impasse that threatened to stop the new nation before it had a chance to begin.

Riding on horseback, Sherman braved a hard, steady rain on Wednesday, May 30, 1787, to take his seat at the Constitutional Convention. The convention was originally intended to simply strengthen the Articles of Confederation that he had helped write. Sherman quickly came to recognize the need for a new government. He supported the rights of the individual states, and he dedicated himself to protecting those rights as the new Constitution was created.

Sherman's peers repeatedly demonstrated how much they respected him, but he also was a shrewd and experienced politician. Connecticut's Jeremiah

Sherman held many public offices during his long political career.

Wadsworth found him to be "cunning as the Devil, and if you attack him, you ought to know him well; he is not easily managed, but if he suspects you are trying to take him in, you may as well catch an eel by the tail."[1]

On Monday, July 2, after countless debates and disagreements, a Grand Committee was named to work out a compromise between the Virginia Plan and the New Jersey Plan. The Virginia Plan was supported by the large states. Smaller states supported the New Jersey Plan.

Oliver Ellsworth was to be Connecticut's representative to the committee, but when it met on Tuesday, July 3, Ellsworth was ill. The sixty-six-year-old Sherman took his place. Sherman offered a compromise form of representative government that pleased both the large and small states and protected the rights of each state. He proposed that the House of Representatives be elected based on state population. This house would have the right to draft all spending and budget bills. In the Senate each state would have an equal vote. In what came to be known as the Great Compromise or the Connecticut Compromise, Sherman freed the political logjam that had brought the Constitutional Convention to a halt. The meeting continued, and a new form of representative government was born.

Sherman was one of only a handful of men to sign the Declaration of Independence, the Articles of Confederation, and the Constitution. His vital contribution to the convention was undeniable. He rose to speak 138 times and provided the necessary guidance when it was most needed.

After signing the new Constitution, Sherman returned to Connecticut. In his slow and hesitating style of speech, he explained the principles of the new form of government to the members of his state's ratifying convention.

As had happened to several other founding fathers, the years of public service took their toll on Sherman's financial well-being. Along with the costs of more than a dozen children, Sherman was inattentive to his private income during his years in public positions. He soon found himself on the brink of financial ruin. Only his income from different public offices allowed him to escape.

Sherman's New Haven was one of a half dozen cities to embrace the new government and celebrate the new Constitution with a paradelike "Federal Procession." His friends and supporters chose to send Sherman back to Congress. They elected him to the new House of Representatives.

On the House floor Sherman joined fellow founding father James Madison in support of Federalist legislation during the first session of the Congress. Sherman supported the creation of the federal court system and the creation of the departments of War, Treasury, and State. Sherman also supported Treasury Secretary Alexander Hamilton's plan to pay off the national debt.

In 1791, the Connecticut legislature paid tribute to the man from New Haven when they appointed him to the United States Senate. Although he maintained his vocal support for the independence and the rights of strong individual states, Sherman continued to vote for Federalist legislation.

Sherman was still his town's mayor and one of his state's senators when he died in New Haven on July 23, 1793. Sherman was one of only a select and unique group of Americans to participate in every stage of the new nation's development. From the Declaration of Independence to the first session of the first Congress, no one else assumed as many responsibilities nor served in as many different roles—both local and national. Sherman truly was a witness to history.

Chapter Notes

Chapter 1. John Adams: The Voice of Independence

1. L. H. Butterfield, ed., *The Adams Papers; Diary & Autobiography of John Adams*, vol. 3 (Cambridge, Mass.: Belknap Press of Harvard University Press, 1961), p. 257.

2. Ibid., p. 259.

3. L. H. Butterfield, ed., *The Adams Papers; Adams Family Correspondence*, vol. 2 (Cambridge, Mass.: Belknap Press of Harvard University Press, 1963), p. 30.

4. Richard B. Morris, *Seven Who Shaped Our Destiny* (New York: Harper & Row, 1973), p. 79.

Chapter 2. Alexander Hamilton: Founding Federalist

1. Harold C. Syrett, *The Papers of Alexander Hamilton*, vol. 1 (New York: Columbia University Press, 1961).

2. Morton J. Frisch, ed., *Selected Writings and Speeches of Alexander Hamilton* (Washington, D.C.: American Enterprise Institute for Public Policy Research, 1985), p. 123.

Chapter 3. John Jay: Reluctant Revolutionary

1. Richard B. Morris, *Witnesses at the Creation* (New York: Holt, Rinehart and Winston, 1985), p. 58.

2. L. H. Butterfield, ed., *The Adams Papers; Adams Family Correspondence*, vol. 1 (Cambridge, Mass.: Belknap Press of Harvard University Press, 1963), p. 156.

3. Richard B. Morris, *Seven Who Shaped Our Destiny* (New York: Harper & Row, 1973), p. 172.

4. Richard B. Morris, *Witnesses at the Creation*, p. 190.

5. Ibid., p. 57.

Chapter 4. Thomas Jefferson: Architect of Democracy

1. William Howard Adams, *Jefferson's Monticello* (New York: Abbeville Press, 1983), frontispiece.

2. Ibid., back cover.

3. Adrienne Koch and William Peden, *The Life and Selected Writings of Thomas Jefferson* (New York: Random House, 1993), p. 10.

4. L.H. Butterfield, ed., *The Adams Papers; Diary & Autobiography of John Adams*, vol. 3 (Cambridge, Mass.: Belknap Press of Harvard University Press, 1961), p. 335.

5. Richard B. Morris, *Seven Who Shaped Our Destiny* (New York: Harper & Row, 1973), p. 107.

6. Joseph J. Ellis, *American Sphinx: The Character of Thomas Jefferson* (New York: Alfred A. Knopf, 1997), p. 26.

7. Ibid., p. 192.

8. Adams, p. 249.

Chapter 5. Richard Henry Lee: Southern Radical

1. Adrienne Koch and William Peden, *The Life and Selected Writings of Thomas Jefferson* (New York: Random House, 1993), p. 16.

2. James Curtis Ballagh, ed., *The Letters of Richard Henry Lee*, vol. 1 (New York: The Macmillan Company, 1911), p. 198.

3. L.H. Butterfield, ed., *The Adams Papers; Diary & Autobiography of John Adams*, vol. 3 (Cambridge: Belknap Press of Harvard University Press, 1961), p. 336,

4. Ballagh, vol. 2, p. 434.

5. Ibid., p. 583.

Chapter 6. James Madison: Father of the Constitution

1. Richard B. Morris, *Witnesses at the Creation* (New York: Holt, Rinehart and Winston, 1985), p. 101.

2. Adrienne Koch and William Peden, *The Life and*

Selected Writings of Thomas Jefferson (New York: Random House, 1993), p. 42.

Chapter 7. George Mason: Father of Virginia's Declaration of Rights

1. William J. Bennett, *Our Sacred Honor* (New York: Simon & Schuster, 1997), p. 93.

2. Adrienne Koch and William Peden, *The Life and Selected Writings of Thomas Jefferson* (New York: Random House, 1993), p. 42.

3. Clinton Rossiter, *1787: The Grand Convention* (New York: W. W. Norton and Company, 1987), p. 226.

4. Robert A. Rutland, ed., *The Papers of George Mason, 1725–1792*, vol. 3 (Chapel Hill: The University of North Carolina Press, 1970), p. 973.

5. Bennett, p. 93.

Chapter 8. Gouverneur Morris: Penman of the Constitution

1. Beatrix Cary Davenport, ed., *A Diary of the French Revolution*, vol. 1 (Westport, Conn.: Greenwood Press, 1972), p. xi.

2. Clinton Rossiter, *1787: The Grand Convention* (New York: W. W. Norton and Company, 1987), p. 225.

3. Howard Swiggert, *The Extraordinary Mr. Morris* (New York: Doubleday & Company, Inc., 1952), p. 225.

Chapter 10. Roger Sherman: Witness to History

1. Clinton Rossiter, *1787: The Grand Convention* (New York: W. W. Norton and Company, 1987), pp. 91–92.

Further Reading

Boardman, R. S. *Roger Sherman: Signer and Statesman.* New York: Da Capo Press, Inc., 1971.

Collier, Christopher, and J. L. Collier. *Building a New Nation, 1789–1803.* Tarrytown, N.Y.: Marshall Cavendish Corporation, 1998.

Dwyer, Frank. *John Adams.* Broomall, Pa.: Chelsea House Publishers, 1989.

Leavell, Perry. *James Madison.* Broomall, Pa.: Chelsea House Publishers, 1988.

Malone, Mary. *James Madison.* Springfield, N.J.: Enslow Publishers, Inc., 1997.

Morris, Richard B. *Seven Who Shaped Our Destiny.* New York: Harper & Row, 1973.

Old, Wendie C. *Thomas Jefferson.* Springfield, N.J.: Enslow Publishers, Inc., 1997.

Pellow, George. *John Jay.* Broomall, Pa.: Chelsea House Publishers, 1980.

Whitelaw, Nancy. *More Perfect Union: The Story of Alexander Hamilton.* Greensboro, N.C.: Morgan Reynolds, Inc., 1997.

Internet Addresses

Archiving Early America
<http://earlyamerica.com>

The historic documents from eighteenth century America posted on this site illuminate life during the founding of the United States.

A Hypertext on American History
<http://odur.let.rug.nl/~usa/index.htm>

This website posted by the University of Groningen in the Netherlands contains presidential biographies and historical documents from the United States Information Agency enriched with links to other documents and websites.

Library of Congress American Memory Project
<http://lcweb2.loc.gov/>

The American Memory Project is a digital library of documents and photos illustrating American history.

National Archives and Records Administration: The Founding Fathers
<http://www.nara.gov/exhall/charters/constitution/ confath.html>

This site contains short biographies of all of the Founding Fathers who attended the Constitutional Convention of 1787. The National Archives website posts numerous documents and biographies.

Index